#NEVERHOMELESS

A MANUAL FOR HOMELESS MINISTRY

Alex Fleming

TRILOGY CHRISTIAN PUBLISHERS

TUSTIN, CA

Trilogy Christian Publishers
A Wholly Owned Subsidary of Trinity Broadcasting Network
2442 Michelle Drive
Tustin, CA 92780

#NEVERHOMELESS

Rights Department, 2442 Michelle Drive, Tustin, CA 92780.

Trilogy Christian Publishing/TBN and colophon are trademarks of Trinity Broadcasting Network.

Cover design by: Beth Harp Photography, Lagrange, Indiana

For information about special discounts for bulk purchases, please contact Trilogy Christian Publishing.

Trilogy Disclaimer: The views and content expressed in this book are those of the author and may not necessarily reflect the views and doctrine of Trilogy Christian Publishing or the Trinity Broadcasting Network.

Manufactured in the United States of America

10 9 8 7 6 5 4 3 2 1

Library of Congress Cataloging-in-Publication Data is available.

ISBN: 978-1-68556-234-2

E-ISBN: 978-1-68556-235-9

#NEVERHOMELESS
A Manual for Homeless Ministry

Life Restored Church
400 Arbor Place, San Antonio, Texas, 78207
Pastor Alex Fleming

Mission: Our mission at Life Restored Church is to restore hope through Jesus Christ to those who feel outcast and dehumanized.

Vision: Our vision is to become a 24/7 church that never closes its doors and acts as a lighthouse to San Antonio. We wish to be the body of Christ and help people overcome their struggles with addiction and homelessness.

This manual should be used as a reference and not a step-by-step guide.
For further questions, contact Alex Fleming at *aflex7@gmail.com*.

A Word from the Pastor

Ministering to the poor and homeless is something that is near to my heart. I grew up in one of the poorest zip codes in San Antonio, Texas and when I was younger, I did a lot of petty crimes. Growing up, many of my friends were either imprisoned or dead, and I knew that sooner or later I would end up the same. So, I went to a community college to try to change my life. During college, I met my wife who introduced me to Christ. After I accepted Christ, I wanted to share the gospel as the Apostle Paul did. So, I married my wife and we moved to Tennessee to attend a Bible college. However, I left after realizing that academia was not the path I needed to take to serve among the poor and homeless. I didn't need a degree. I just needed a heart.

After returning to San Antonio in 2012, my wife and I started a Bible study which then inspired us to start a church. People advised me to plant my church in a more affluent area, such as the suburbs. However, I felt called by God to return to the area where I grew up and show them what a life surrendered to Christ looks like.

When we started Life Restored Church, I didn't take in the homeless at first. It was only after I heard someone had frozen to death that I felt God calling me to take in the homeless. I had no clue how to start, but I knew I needed to do something. One Sunday, I decided to take in the homeless as temperatures were going to drop below freezing. During that time, I challenged pastors around the area to either take in the homeless as well or assist us in our endeavor. We took in the homeless for three days in a row, and I heard the Holy Spirit ask me, "What would Jesus do if he owned your building?" From that point on, I heard a calling and vision from God to create a 24/7 church, where we minister to the homeless through all hours of the day.

Thank you for your interest in starting an inner-city homeless ministry. The purpose of this ministry is to introduce the homeless to Jesus Christ, help them find employment, and get them off the street. We have learned to build trust and create an atmosphere of restoration by ministering to them in love consistently. In three years, we have helped seventeen people get off the streets and into their own homes.

The purpose of this manual is to help other ministries reach out to the homeless and share the love of

Christ. I want to give you some insight and advice to help you get started. It is not as impossible as you think. There will be tough days, but by praying consistently and by looking to God for strength and guidance, you can achieve this goal. I want to help you make the biggest dent in homelessness your city has ever seen.

Pastor Alex Fleming

Testimonies

The power of Christ is best shown through people's stories, so we have compiled a few testimonies from our friends at Life Restored Church. You will read three stories in this section: one from a person who got off the streets, one from a person who is on the way to getting off the streets, and one from a person who has received healing.

Mike's Story

We first met Mike through one of our shower ministries. He was reserved, shy, and reluctant to talk to people. When we sat down with him, he asked us why we were providing showers and clothes to people. So, we shared our faith with him. Overwhelmed by our hospitality and kindness, he began to cry. Mike began to volunteer at our church, and we welcomed him with open arms. Eventually, one of our church members became his discipler and encouraged him to get a job.

After a couple of weeks, Mike landed a job and began to take control of his life again. Three months later, he walked into our church with tears in his eyes and the keys to his new apartment. He was overwhelmed by how God had taken him off the streets and into his own home.

Phyllis's Story

About a year ago, we had the privilege of meeting Phyllis through our breakfast ministry. Phyllis is a remarkable and bright woman who saw a lot of potential in our breakfast program. She began to volunteer with us every week, helping us serve breakfast to hundreds of people. She has become one of our most faithful volunteers. She says that serving at Life Restored Church has become her life and purpose, and that the members of our church have become her family. By God's grace, she now has a steady income and is on her way to owning her own home.

Justin's Story

We met Justin just a few months ago while he was on drugs and on the streets. Some members from our church prayed for him, and he was soon healed, not only from his sickness but also from his drug addiction. He has recently received a housing assignment and is on his way towards a new life. He says that prayer and support from Life Restored Church was vital for his transformation.

Contents

1

The Why?

Did you know that serving the poor, homeless, downtrodden and marginalized is mentioned 2/3's more in the Bible than worship? Well, it is. Just google how many times is worship mentioned in the Bible then google how many times is helping the poor mentioned in the Bible and you will have the answer. I believe that is because from worship we are recharged to go out into the world and serve the least of these. I remember my friend gave me a great insight into Matthew 6:25. The scripture states in the NIV, "Therefore I tell you, do not worry about your life, what you will eat or drink; or about your body, what you will wear. Is not life more than food, and the body more than clothes?"

Only non-affluent people are worried about what they will eat or if they will have the basic necessity of clothes to wear. This group of people that Jesus was talking to were poor. Actually, the majority of the people Jesus ministered to were poor. I have always said that only the American Church can turn a physical need into a spiritual need, so they don't have to meet a physical need. The apostle James makes this clear in James 2:15-17 (NIV), "Suppose a brother or a sister is without clothes and daily food. If one of you says to them, 'Go in peace; keep warm and well fed,' but does nothing about their physical needs, what good is it? In the same way, faith by itself if it is not accompanied by action, is dead."

Israel was an occupied nation. Occupied by the Roman government. We must remember that there was no middle class in Jerusalem at the time of Jesus. There was the Roman ruling class, the religious ruling class, the tax collectors and then everyone else. Everyone else was either dirt poor or outcast from society all together. This is the context of Jesus's teachings, miracles, and the majority of His audience. This was not only the case for Jerusalem, but it was so for every city ruled by the Roman Empire. (Go to appendix to read source)

Here is a snapshot of the type of poverty in Jesus's time.

1. Imperial elites: consisting of 0.04% of the population: imperial dynasty, Roman senatorial families, a few retainers, local royalty, and a few freed persons.

2. Regional or provincial elites (1%): equestrian families, provincial officials, some retainers,

some decurial families, some freed persons, some retired military officers.

3. Municipal elites (1.76%): most decurial families, wealthy men and women who do not hold office, some freed persons, some retainers, some veterans, some merchants.

4. Moderate surplus resources (7% estimated): some merchants, some traders, some freed persons, some artisans (especially those who employ others) and military veterans.

5. Stable near subsistence level with reasonable hope of remaining above the minimum lever to sustain life (22% estimated): many merchants and traders, regular wage earners, artisans, large shop owners, freed persons, and some farm families.

6. At subsistence level and often below minimum level to sustain life (40%): small farm families, laborer's (skilled and unskilled), artisans (especially those employed by others), wage earners, most merchants and traders, small shop or tavern owners.

7. Below subsistence level (28%): some farm families, unattached widows, orphans, beggars, disabled, unskilled day laborers, and prisoners.

Jesus was even born in homeless circumstances. Jesus even self identifies as homeless. One of the Apostolic mandates found in Galatians 2:9-10 was to help the poor. With such an emphasis on the homeless and poor from our Lord why has the Church in America downplayed the attention we are supposed to be giving to the poor? Don't get me wrong we do give the poor attention, but it is very marginalized. It has become a hit it and quit it ministry in most churches. We outreach to the poor during the holidays or whatever is the next serving fade that everyone else is doing. Other than that, it's back to the spiritual social club.

It is proven that the bulk of Jesus's ministry was to the poor. This is the reason why I have dedicated my life to restoring the hearts of the pastors back to the poor. I believe based off of biblical scriptures that that is the heart of God. All through the old and new testaments I can sum up the heart of God into these four categories, the lost, the poor, the orphan, and the widow.

The majority of every great revival had a connection to helping the poor. From the first and second great awakenings of the 1700's, to the Azuza street revival, to Billy Graham crusades to the Jesus Movement. There is a formula there. Well, actually it is found in the book of Isaiah chapter 58. For the most part the majority of Christians focus on Isaiah 58:12 (NIV), "Your people will rebuild the ancient ruins and will raise up the age-old foundations; you will be called repairer of broken walls, restorer of streets with dwellings."

But if we only focus on that part of the scripture then it is like putting the cart before the horse. You don't get Isaiah 58:12 until you do Isaiah 58:6-7;10. It's like trying to bake a cake only half the ingredients and expecting it to come out completely the way it was designed to. It doesn't work that way. You have to follow the directions in its proper order. Trust me, I did not know this before. Until 2016 when I had to live this out. When our church did our first winter shelter and started a movement in our city.

It was a cold Sunday morning in San Antonio Texas. Our church is located less than two blocks from the city's funded homeless shelter. As I was in the middle of giving the Sunday morning church announcements, I felt the holy spirit speak a definitive word to me. He said, "You are going to take in the homeless overnight into your church today." It was a cold winter that year and I heard a story of a homeless person dying in the freezing cold overnight. I looked at the congregation of about a hundred people and said, "The Holy Spirit just spoke to me and told me to do something, and I am kind of scared." The look on the congregations' faces were looks of concern. I told them, "I understand that look on your faces but I'm also understanding right now what the Apostle Paul meant when he said, 'I am a slave of Jesus Christ.' I have no choice in the matter. I immediately walked outside as the congregation followed me, I went Facebook live and did the take your shirt off challenge. The challenge was to pastors. It went like this: If you cannot be in this cold weather without your shirt for three minutes, imagine the homeless that have to live in this all night, so either open your churches to take in the homeless or help us take them in.

The video spread and the local news caught wind of it and did a story on it that same day. Pastor takes his shirt off to help the homeless was what the news called it. We cancelled service that day and started moving chairs and stacking them out of the way in preparation for bring in the least of these into our church. The citizens of San Antonio immediately started donating blankets, jackets, pillows, sleeping bags. As they were bringing all these items to our church, I realized quickly that just receiving these items was going to be a full-time job. The stage was literally full and stacked to the ceiling with all these donations.

I thought the homeless was one big gang that were going to assault me and steal all our music equipment. That was so not the case, at all. People that saw the news story started coming to our church to volunteer with facilitating and preparing meals. We made some generic flyers and passed them out to every homeless person we ran into. We had food donated and at 6 p.m. that same Sunday night we were ready to take them in.

We checked in all their luggage and did a mild search for any weapons or drugs. Yes, the homeless have luggage. Well, it's more like their whole life in those bags and back packs. After everyone got in and was seated on their sleeping bags, we passed out the food and prayed. We had a Christmas movie playing on the T.V. I think it was the movie *Elf*. To my surprise, about 95% of the people feel asleep around 9 p.m. That was pretty early for me, and I was surprised.

Later as I got better acquainted with this type of lifestyle, I learned that being in the sun and cold all day and walking all day puts a toil on your body and after a good meal you fall right asleep.

After all the volunteers had left it was just me and two other guys who pulled the overnight shift. Guess what? No one robbed us, not everyone in the church knew each other. They weren't a big gang. Actually, the homeless helped us keep order with other homeless who were a little antagonistic. Turns out that they really were grateful to us for opening our doors. We had about twenty-five people show up that first night. Thirty-five the second night and by the fourth night fifty people had a warm shelter to stay in. I cannot believe that was the first time that I really made an extreme effort to help the homeless. I mean, as a pastor, you would think this is what we think of doing all the time. But that is not the case at all. We pastors get caught up in sermon series, memorable quotes to give, how much tithe is coming in to pay the bills. All of these are important and needed, but Jesus just finds helping the poor more important.

After the winter shelter, we had hosted was finished I felt like giving myself a big pat on the back. Then the Lord spoke to me again. He said, "If Jesus owned your building, He wouldn't be satisfied with two Sunday morning services and a mid-week service. That birthed the vision for a 24/7 church. There is an old Tanzanian proverb that I live by, "Little by little a little became a lot." And that's how we went from serving and ministering to the homeless from once a week to six days a week. We have seen an average of five homeless people a year get saved, get jobs and get into their own apartments, we have had 14,000 volunteer hours annually, 1,000 sleeping bags given out each year, 2,400 showers provided, 900 volunteers and 19,200 meals served each year.

During one winter shelter, I came across a man who touched my heart. He was one of the people spending the night at our winter shelter. During intake we ask everyone staying to empty out their pockets so we can make sure no has anything illegal on them before entering in. Turns out he had some pills without a prescription. I told him he couldn't stay unless I got rid of the pills. It was obvious to me the pills where illegal drugs. He said he was, "not giving up his pills." I said, "then you can't stay." He looked over my shoulder to see the movie we had playing. The movie was (It's a Wonderful Life) you know that classic Christmas movie starring Jimmy Stewart. He said, "I really like this movie." He gave up the pills and made his way to the alter of the church close to where the TV monitors were. Towards the end of the movie, he began to sob. I don't know if that movie reminded him of what life was like before he became homeless, but that man continued coming to church afterwards. He got saved, got a job, and got himself an apartment. That's just one story of how God uses acts of love and kindness to save and restore lives.

Fast forward five years and Texas received the worst winter in our history.

2

The Four Levels of Inner-City Churches

As an inner-city church, we strive to constantly improve our ministry to the poor and homeless. Our goal is to be a complete home and refuge to these people. We have created a four-level system for describing the number of services inner-city churches provide. Being at different levels does not mean one church is better than the other; it just means they are at different points in the journey of ministering to the homeless.

Level 1 Churches are inner-city churches that provide basic needs, such as food, showers, toiletries, and clothing 1-3 times a week.

Level 2 Churches provide the same basic needs 5 or more times a week.

Level 3 Churches are the same as Level 2 Churches, except they also provide shelter in the case of inclement weather, such as extreme cold or severe thunderstorms. Life Restored Church is currently a Level 3 Church, but our goal is to become a Level 4 Church.

A **Level 4 Church** does all the above, except they also provide daily overnight shelter and programs to detoxify and rehabilitate.

3

Getting Started

When starting a homeless ministry, we suggest serving a pancake breakfast once a week. After that becomes popular, you can start serving breakfast and other meals more frequently. In this section, we explain how to recruit volunteers, make the foods on our menu, recruit restaurants for catering, deliver our "Zero Aggression Speech," and compose your outside and inside crews.

2.1. Recruiting Volunteers

If your church cannot provide enough manpower to host a pancake breakfast, you may want to recruit volunteers. One way to recruit volunteers is by asking other churches to commit to volunteering once a month for six months. Since this is a low commitment, it will ease volunteers into the ministry. However, consistency is crucial. If volunteers are not able to come on a regular basis, then we suggest waiting until they can commit. You want consistent volunteers so you can avoid scrambling to find manpower. Volunteer teams should be between eight and twenty people.

Another way to recruit volunteers is through social media, such as Facebook. When using this method, you must describe the work that needs to be done and the positions that must be filled. The positions for a pancake breakfast are:

- Welcomers: 2 people welcoming people into the church (see 2.5. Outside Crew and 2.6. Inside Security/Watchmen)
- Drinks: 2 people preparing and serving drinks.
- Cooks: 1 person preparing the pancake mix and 2 people cooking the pancakes.
- Preparation: 1 person preparing plates and utensils.
- Servers: 3-4 people serving the plates and utensils.

The number of people for each position should be adjusted based on how big your space is and how many guests are coming.

Other groups you can contact for volunteers are local college ministries and missionary groups. Missionary groups tend to be more common during the summer, so we suggest recruiting them during that time, especially since church attendance is usually low. You can recruit them by advertising on social media and by reaching out to associations and organizations. Life Restored Church is a part of the San Antonio Baptist Association (SABA). To recruit missionary groups, we contacted the missions/outreach director of SABA who then reached out to the other organizations of the association. Missionary groups can help with your regular services and other projects you may have in progress, such as painting a house, building a fence, and more. Missionary groups also usually cover any expenses with their work.

If possible, try to have all your supplies provided by other churches and organizations to reduce your expenses. In this way, they are also investing in the Kingdom of God. For volunteers that show up individually or without a group, your church will need to provide the supplies.

2.2. Menu

This section includes the recipes for our menu items. Our recipes are made to serve about a hundred people and each meal is served with coffee, water, and occasionally orange juice. You will need about ten gallons of coffee and five gallons of orange juice per day. Make sure you have enough bowls/plates, cups, silverware, napkins, and aluminum foil/saran wrap (for when guests take their food to go).

Coffee

We have learned that people who are recovering from alcohol and drug addiction prefer their coffee to be sweet. The coffee recipe that has satisfied our guests and our serving instructions can be found in Figure 1.

1.) 80 cup coffee makers - We have TWO. One is missing the on/off switch but is "ON" once plugged in.

  * **4-5 cups of coffee grounds maximum**

(After one or two pitchers of coffee have been dispensed you can add a full pitcher of water back into the grounds and/or pot)

2.) Pre-mix coffee with creamer and sugar. (And then serve them at their seat) - Use large plastic pitchers to serve coffee for pancake breakfasts, weekday breakfast and other events. This helps with traffic and inventory control.

  * Use 12 oz styrofoam cups
  * Please have visitor's keep their cups for refills

PER GALLON PITCHER MIX

1 CUP SUGAR + 1 CUP CREAMER

or 1½ of each

Pancake Breakfast

Figure 1: Coffee Recipe

Use 2x10 lb. bags of premade pancake mix and 3-4 electric skillets to prepare the pancakes. Supplement the pancakes with 100 pieces of bacon or ham.

Oatmeal and Cinnamon Toast

Use 4x42 oz containers of quick oats for the oatmeal. Add 16 oz of raisins to the oatmeal and add cinnamon to taste. Have milk and sugar available upon request.

Use 300 slices of white bread for the cinnamon toast. Butter both sides and cook over 3-4 electric griddles. In a bowl, mix cinnamon and sugar, adding slightly more sugar than cinnamon. Sprinkle over both sides of cooked bread.

Breakfast Tacos

We make three types of tacos: chorizo and egg, egg and potato, and bean and cheese. Use a total of 300 flour tortillas.

For the chorizo and egg tacos, use 5x12 eggs and 3 lbs. of chorizo. Cook both together over a stove.

For the egg and potato tacos, use 5x12 eggs and 5 lbs. of tater tots, thawed. Cook both together over a stove, crushing the tater tots.

For the bean and cheese tacos, use 2x6.6 lbs. cans of refried beans and 2 lbs. of shredded cheese (either Cheddar or Mexican blend). Cook the beans over a stove, and when wrapping the tacos, add cheese.

2.3. Recruiting Restaurants

Restaurants play a vital role in helping run a homeless ministry. Restaurants can contribute in two ways.

First, they can donate a complete meal (i.e., 100 meals) once a week. Las Chiladas is one of our key partners who helped us start our breakfast ministry. They have committed to donating breakfast tacos every Monday. Second, restaurants can donate food as a supplement to the food you already have. We contacted local donut restaurants and asked them to donate their leftover donuts to serve alongside our regular menu.

An important thing to consider is if a restaurant can offer their support and resources consistently, not sporadically. We suggest inviting local restaurants to partner with you for three or six months at a time.

2.4. The Zero Aggression Speech

We have provided a template of our Zero-Aggression Speech below. We deliver this speech at the beginning of each service we provide to clearly communicate to our guests our intentions.

"Thank you, guys, for coming to (church name). We're glad that you're here, and we want to serve you guys and show you the love of Christ. Thank you for being here. We tolerate ZERO aggression in the House of God. All we ask is that you show us the same respect that we are showing you. If you have any beef with someone out on the street, please do not let it come inside this church. If you feel as if you must handle something, I do not condone or recommend this, but please leave the premises of this church and its surrounding areas."

This is just an example of what to say, but the general message should be the same. An additional thing to consider is word choice; use language that is easily understood.

2.5. Outside Crew

The outside crew is responsible for making sure there is no trouble outside of the church where people are gathering. These members must be able to walk in love but also be able to assert themselves. They have to be able to discern and identify high risk people. They have the responsibility to determine who to let into the church for the safety of others.

These members have the duty of exhibiting PTA to the utmost degree. They also have the responsibility that the guests are lined up in an orderly fashion for when the doors open. They must always be on the lookout for signs of physical or verbal aggression. If there is aggression, they need to handle the situation by restating the zero-aggression policy and ready to apply the PTA de-escalation process. You want to make sure that the people waiting in line for your service are waiting in your designated area and not trespassing on others property. Another thing that the outside crew can do is hand out umbrellas to protect the guests from the extreme sun or from the rain. As the guest comes in, they return the umbrellas before they can receive the service.

2.6. Inside Security/Watchmen

These people are constantly in contact with the outside crew and perform much of the same duties. Their duties are also incredibly important. This person is the host and gives instructions and announcements. They run the flow of the inside with directions. While doing this, this person is constantly aware and on the lookout for signs of verbal or physical aggression. They also must be watching to make sure no transactions of drugs happen. Another thing that the inside watchman can be in control of is the indoor bathroom. They can run security on the bathroom so that no transactions or illegal activities occur in the bathroom. This is just an additional measure that the church can undertake. At the Life Restored Church, we do not have an open public bathroom as we do not have the staff to manage that.

4

The De-escalation Process

In a perfect world, a church and its members would never have to undergo de-escalation processes in the event of an aggressive or belligerent person. However, this is unfortunately not the case, so we have developed a process in order to quickly and efficiently de-escalate a situation that promotes the most love and an ending leaving both parties not upset.

4.1. Proactive, Not Reactive

One of the first steps is to be proactive instead of being reactive. We can be proactive by setting an environment of peace, love, and welcomeness through encouraging greetings and words of affirmation along with handshakes and smiles. You can also greet the homeless by praying for them and talking to them if they are waiting around. Another thing that can be put in place is to have a host or emcee who sets the tone of the room.

Their duties could include letting them know how the situation is going to work, the order of events, where to get things, house rules etc. On the mic they can talk about how our church has a zero-aggression policy and that we are a loving church that respects everyone. We are not waiting for something bad to happen first in order to react to it, but instead creating an environment where we would not have to react to a negative situation in the first place.

> **Volunteer:** *"Hello! Good morning and God bless."*
> *"How are you doing today?"*
> *"How may I pray for you today?"*
> *"Is there anything I can get for you?"*

> **Host:** *"Hey everyone! I hope everyone is doing well today. Coffee is over there, and we will be handing out food shortly if you could find a seat."*
> *"Again, we have a zero-aggression policy. We do not tolerate aggression or violence here. We love one another and respect each other as people."*

4.2. PTA: Please, Thank You, Apologize

A gentle answer turns away wrath, but a harsh word stirs up anger. Proverbs 15:1 (NIV)

In the event of aggression in the form of words or body language, there are steps we can take to quickly de-escalate the situation and leave everyone more at peace. We call this the PTA Method: Please, Thank you, Apologize, or more applicably the ATP method.

After coming into contact with aggression, we first apologize for any inconvenience that they may have experienced. We then thank them for their patience, and then tell them that we are going to complete the request and/or make a request of our own accompanied with a please.

A key point to all of these is that the conversation is carried out with a calm confidence that is assertive but not aggressive. We use "sir" and "ma'am" when addressing people, no matter who they are. We do not want to provide an avenue for the person to take advantage of our "non-aggression", but we also do not want to provoke more anger. A few scenarios can help explain this further.

(All of the following scenarios could involve a variety of parties and situations. These are just a set of hypotheticals.)

Scenario 1: Person Does Not Like the Coffee

> **Homeless person:** *"Hey man! This coffee sucks. I hate this, get this out of here."* Volunteer: *"Sir I* **apologize** *for that, I'm sorry for any inconvenience it may have caused.* **Thank you** *for your patience*

*with this. If you could **please** let me know how I could fix this for you I would love to do that. Again, thank you for your patience."*

In this case, the aggression present was not very serious and had an easy solution. So, the appropriate response was to PTA and complete the request as best possible.

Scenario 2: Person Says Food is Cold, Becomes Belligerent

> **Homeless person:** *(aggressive body language)* "Hey!! What are you guys doing?!? This stuff is awful man, why are you serving this garbage to us. You guys are useless... etc."
> **Volunteer:** *(Confident and assertive tone and body language)* "Sir. Please calm down. Again, we tolerate zero aggression. I **apologize** that this happened to you and **thank you** for your patience with this. If you could **please** wait while I look into fixing this for you, I would appreciate that."

This difference between this scenario and the first one is that the person is displaying an aggressive body language and has the potential to escalate. The key here is, when responding, to display confidence and authoritative power. Even though they are not displaying patience, saying that they will catch them off guard and maybe in fact cause them to listen.

Scenario 3: Still Not Listening

> **Homeless person:** *(after initial requests)* *could take a variety of forms including expletives and even more aggressive body language*
> **Volunteer:** *"Sir. Please calm down. If you do not calm down or leave, I will have to call the police to escort you from the premises." *fakes phone call**

In this scenario, it has escalated to the point where words probably could not cause them to calm down. Our way of dealing with this is to fake a phone call to the police. The reason we initially fake the phone call is to not actually bother the police with many minor problems that probably do not really need police intervention. We want a healthy relationship with the police department. Ways to fake a phone call to the police is to put the phone on silent and take a couple steps away. Say things such as describing the perpetrator, saying the location, asking how near the nearest officer is and such in a loud voice. In most cases, the aggressive person will take the hint and leave.

One of the reasons that this method works is that it flips the narrative of aggression. Many of these people are used to having aggression responded to with more aggression that quickly escalates into a toxic and often violent confrontation. Responding with patience, understanding, and love often leaves them confused and less likely to become violent. Many times, in Scripture is it said to be slow to anger and to respond with love (James 1:19, Matthew 5:9, Proverbs 14:29, Psalms 37:8).

4.5. The Invitation to the Homeless

The first thing you should do is to target the homeless population in your local area. In general, the highest density of homelessness in a city will be within a three-mile radius of your city's homeless shelter. Once you have identified where your city's homeless population is, make flyers inviting the homeless to a "FREE PANCAKE BREAKFAST." Be sure to include the day and the location, and if possible, include a map for ease of navigation. Try and pass them out in person and **be memorable**, which can include being funny or even being just plain loud. When getting started, you want to pass out flyers the day before and the day of. The day before, try and pass out the flyers later in the day before nightfall. On the day of, hand them out very early in the morning, reminding people that your event is going on. After a month or two of doing it every Saturday, the word spreads and flyers won't be necessary. After a month and a half, try and have a pancake breakfast without passing out flyers and see if you need them anymore.

5

Winter Overnight Shelter

Here are some tips and advice for providing an overnight shelter:

1. Your church is potentially the perfect place to host a winter overnight shelter! If you do not have an open area like a gymnasium, take out all the chairs and tables in the sanctuary, and procure sleeping bags (through social media requests like a sleeping bag drive or just by purchasing them). The size of your space will determine how many people you can fit safely.

   a. Because of limited space, take them on a first-come basis.

2. Our church uses tickets, which serves as their pass to stay the night. We hand out the tickets two hours

ahead of time, so people don't have to wait in line for too long. Once they have a ticket, their spot is secured.

    a. The ticket should be something that they cannot duplicate to prevent fraud.

3. Once the guests are inside, it's important to figure out a way to track their luggage.

    a. At our church, the person will give their luggage to us.

    b. We'll label the luggage with masking tape and give them a ticket with the corresponding number.

    c. At this point, we tell the person to grab what they need from their baggage, since their luggage won't be accessible until the morning.

    d. A runner will receive the luggage and put it into a designated storage area. Make sure that the storage area is in a place where only staff can access it.

4. Make sure to have ushers who lead people to the sleeping area. If possible, try to keep the genders separate.

5. If possible, prepare food before people get admitted into the shelter - this way food can be served as they come in. It may be efficient to have the homeless sit

on their sleeping bag and for the servers bring them food.

   a. During this time, servers should pick up trash.

   b. If your church has screens, it may be a good idea to put on some movies.

6. Once they come in and sit down, there should be as little moving around as possible. Encourage the homeless to simply sit, eat, then sleep.

7. Inside the sleeping area, there should be one or two people watching the room and making sure nothing violent or offensive happens. This can be done in shifts so that nobody must stay up all night. At least two people are needed to watch the room while someone goes outside to smoke - one goes outside to smoke while the other stays inside.

8. We wake them up around 6 a.m. with breakfast, which should be donated or cooked beforehand.

5.1 Exit Strategy

When it is time to clean up or close, it can be difficult to get people moving out in a timely manner. The key to ushering people out efficiently, is to approach them with love and respect. Keeping a lighthearted tone is vital. Here are some recommended steps to ushering people out:

1. Have the host lead off with something like, "Hey guys! Five more minutes and then we're gonna be shutting down. Glad y'all could be here!" This communicates to people that it is almost time to leave.

2. Once it is time to leave, say, "Okay guys, we're closing. If you could start making your way to the door that would be great!"

3. For those that didn't hear or got caught up in something, after several minutes say, "Hey guys just a reminder that we're closed down now. Anybody sitting down, if you could stand up for me and make your way to the door, that'd be great." At this point most people should be out, and individual people can be talked to and subtly ushered out.

4. A good thing to do is to directly invite them to the next event so that they feel not as if they were being kicked out, but just waiting for the next event.

6

Shower Service

Providing showers and clothing is a great way to serve the homeless community. Many homeless go days without showers. By providing showers to the homeless, you are also keeping them happy, healthy, and clean. Below is an example of how a shower ministry can function.

You should assign these roles while running a shower ministry:

- **Scribe:** The scribe writes down each person's order as they enter. They are the first volunteer that they encounter, so their job is also to set the atmosphere for the guests.

- **Runner:** The runner takes each order to the closest to become assembled and takes out the specified clothing order.

- **Clothing assemblers:** The clothing assemblers fulfill the orders from the cards that are brought to them from the runner.

- **Security:** Security ensures safety by making the people empty out their pockets into a designated safe area that security will watch continuously. They also watch over the belongings while people are showering.

- At least two **Timers:** There should be at least two timers, one female timer for when females shower and one male timer for when males shower. The timers will guide the guests to the showers, notify them of how much time they have, and give them a 2-minute warning.

- **Overseer:** The overseer watches over everyone and makes sure that everything is running smoothly. They also call out the order number and names when it is their time to shower.

Here is the process for providing showers:

1. When someone walks in, we fill out a form consisting of their name, gender, pant size, shirt size, and additional requests they may make (underwear, socks, etc.)

a. There are two types of forms that we can fill out - one for showers, and one for clothes. The shower form will have a call number.

2. After we fill out the form, he/she should take a seat and wait until his/her name is called. While the guest is waiting, encourage volunteers to talk to them and to ask about their stories. This is a great way to help the homeless people pass the time, especially if they are waiting for a long time.

3. From there, the runners will deliver the form to the closet. In the closet, they should fulfill the ticket order to the best of their ability and include a hygiene pack and a towel.

4. It may be efficient to designate a part of the room as a "transition zone." In this area, we keep the complete clothing orders.
   a. Only people whose names are called to go shower are allowed in this area. We do not give people clothes or let them handle the clothes until right before they head into the showers to avoid theft.

5. Your church should designate someone to watch people's possessions. Before someone enters the showers, we have them empty their pockets and

leave their belongings in a container. We take this precaution because people may do illegal activities, such as smuggling drugs, in the showers. Additionally, it is a good way to insure people do not lose their possessions.

6. The showers last eight minutes, which is timed by a male when males are showering and a female when females are showering. There is a two-minute warning during the eight minutes. If they are not out in eight minutes, there is a one-minute grace period before the water is manually shut off.

   a. We verbally reinforce the urgency to clear the shower stalls so that we can send the next group in before turning the water back on so that they can finish up. If they still do not leave the water is shut off permanently.

7. After the shower, they are welcome to leave. They should drop off their towel in a bin so they can be washed later.

   a. For us, our shower ministry lasts from 10:30 a.m. to 12:00 p.m., but we stop letting people in at 11:45 a.m. Around this same time, we gently usher those that have already taken a shower out of the space, using similar exit strategies to the ones listed in this manual.

8. We do not allow in and out movement because people who come in right before the end of the shower ministry time will actually finish well past the actual end time.

    a. Once people have filled out the ticket order, they should stay inside the church. If someone does leave, we do not allow them back in. This is to prevent extraneous traffic and transactions occurring.

9. Some additional things that can be done to bolster the shower ministry is to provide snacks while they wait and a simple sack lunch to take with them after they leave.

7

Clothing Closet

Our closet is stocked entirely through donations, which is accomplished through clothing drives, social media campaigns, and word of mouth. Clothes that are donated must be washed or brand new because homeless people deserve fresh clothes as well. The essentials for both genders are pants, t-shirts, shorts, socks, undergarments, towels, and hygiene packs. When you first begin, just take in all the donations you can. Yet, as you continue your ministry, you may want to see the demographics and needs of people so that you can ask for certain sizes. As for your closet, we recommend that you divide your closet into male and female and organize the clothes by size. This will help fulfill the ticket orders in a timely manner.

Hygiene packs consist of basics such as one-time use or travel size shampoo, conditioner, toothpaste and toothbrush, and lotion. Additional items like sunscreen, deodorant, and razors can also be included.

8

Risk Level Metric System

The Risk Level Metric System is a way to categorize people based on their potential risk to the church and its guests and staff.

- **Risk level 1** is someone who is quiet, compliant, and causes no trouble whatsoever.
- **Risk level 2** is someone who is intoxicated or under the influence but compliant.
- **Risk level 3** is someone who is intoxicated or mentally ill and is displaying erratic behavior. If a person is intoxicated or displaying mental illness, let them in at your own discretion.
- **Risk level 4** is someone whose behavior is aggravating other members. This can be due to intoxication, aggressiveness, or mental conditions.
- **Risk level 5** is someone who is known to be a fighter and is aggressive. A person who is seen

to be a trigger to others for whatever reason, are placed at a level 5.

In general, you will mostly encounter levels 1 to 2, and several level 3s. With levels 3 through 5, it is best to keep an eye on them and be ready to de-escalate. If Level 4s and 5s do act in a way that is not conducive to a healthy environment in the church, then temporary bans can be placed on them, depending on the degree of the offense and the discretion of the pastor. If anyone, no matter the level, puts hands on or strikes volunteers or staff, will be permanently banned.

9

Fundraising

Fundraising may seem overwhelming at first, but it is important to not give up. When we began this ministry, we were faithful to ask people to give. Even though we started small, we were able to develop relationships with other pastors and to ask for more. From personal experience, we have found that ministry does not follow money, but that money follows ministry.

A good first step is to set up electronic donations, so it is easier for people to give. Our church uses "Clovergive," which is our main influx of money.

A good way to build connections is to use social media; social media has been integral for funding our ministry and developing new financial partnerships. We upload pictures and videos of our outreaches consistently on our Facebook page, so people can see what they are donating to. It's important that people can see what your ministry is doing, so that they will be encouraged and compelled to give more.

Below is an example on how to ask others to give:

Hello Pastor, we are raising money with our BBQ plate sale to expand our shower ministry by adding 1 to 2 new shower stalls. The estimated cost is $12,000. We are also looking to raise money for a full-time staff member, (Blank), who is ordained by Life Restored Church. Our goal for him is $30,000. Would you and your church be interested in purchasing barbecue plates? Plates are $8.00 and they include chicken, sausages, rice, beans, and potato salad. The barbecue date is (blank). When we reach our goal, we would have the capacity to do more than what we are currently doing for the homeless! Each ticket is like placing $8 into the hands of a homeless person who is going to benefit from it more than you can imagine! Thank you for your consideration, please get back to me. Thanks again!

If you need more help with fundraising, email *aflex7@gmail.com*. Fundraising is most of the time an identity issue. Do not be too proud to ask for money. Giving donations is biblical.

1 0

Bikes, Wheelchairs, and Dogs

Some of our guests will occasionally have larger and more valuable possessions, such as bikes, wheelchairs, dogs, and other items. We want to be able to accommodate everyone, so having a system of managing these possessions without cluttering your serving space is vital.

You must have a ticket and tagging system in order to label their possessions. This system is similar to storing possessions during the overnight winter shelter. If your church is not wheelchair or bike accessible, then you should bring the food out to them or construct wheelchair accessibility. Dogs are not allowed inside of the building if food is being served. Try your best to accommodate your guests as much as possible.